Real Estate Investing For Beginners

Quick and Easy Beginner's Guide to Successfully Securing Financing, Building Wealth Through Real Estate To Create a Financial Freedom

Robert Zone

Table of contents

The information in the following pages is broadly considered a truthful and accurate account of facts and as such, any inattention, use, or misuse of the information in question by the reader will render any resulting actions solely under their purview. There are no scenarios in which the publisher or the original author of this work can be in any fashion deemed liable for any hardship or damages that may befall them after undertaking information described herein.

Additionally, the information in the following pages is intended only for informational purposes and should thus be thought of as universal. As befitting its nature, it is presented without assurance regarding its prolonged validity or interim quality. Trademarks that are mentioned are done without written consent and can in no way be considered an endorsement from the trademark holder.

Introduction

Real estate is an investment, not only in money but in time. Yes, it can provide stability, and regular returns if done correctly. But before all that can take place, you need to engage in some serious introspection. What made you first look at one deal over another? Is this something you need or want? Will this produce the monetary and potentially emotional returns you were hoping? Will this deal require any sacrifices, such as relocation, or a lot of extra time?

You don't even need to directly own real estate in order for this to happen.

Moreover, your income from real estate investments is not affected by inflation. If anything, your rental income will increase along with inflation. This means that you will be able to enjoy a higher cash flow while maintaining or improving the purchasing power of your money.

There are tax benefits too. If you have investment property, you are allowed to deduct deprecation of the building and any additional capital investments, which will reduce your taxable income. And there are other tax advantages you can enjoy based on what investment method you use.

While this all may sound a little 'woo' to you, the reality is that you have to know what you want and why you want it. Knowing these things comes with understanding who you are. Do a little soul searching to discover your true beliefs and values. What is that you truly hold dear, to run a business and understand your boundaries and belief system and values take work and a deep knowing of you who you are. If this isn't something you've ever done or considered it won't be easy. But it will separate the successful business owners from the unsuccessful ones.

In this book, we will describe the various methods that you can use to invest in real estate. Like we said before, you don't actually need to be a direct owner of property in order to make money from it. We will give you an overview of each investment method, including the pros and cons of each one. You can also earn your ticket to financial freedom when you learn how real estate investing works. While it is true that real estate is a great investment opportunity, when you lack the wisdom and knowledge about how to operate it, things might turn sour. The game of real estate involves a lot of capital and brain. If you have the capital without the brain, you will commit financial suicide.

Yet, a brain without the capital will lead you nowhere. Therefore, you want to learn how real estate investing works and how to raise money to build a strong investment empire. This will start with your mindset, traits, and values. When you have the mental thought pattern of highly successful real estate investors, you will be able to weather the storms and do well financially.

Ideally, you can make money in real estate either through the capital gains system or cash flow. When you invest in real estate for capital gains, you buy, fix, and sell properties. However, when you invest in cash flow, you invest in buying, holding and collecting rent. The rent will be collected and then used to pay down for other real estate properties while using leverage.

Through effective property management systems, the value of the property will be increased over time. This will enable you to pay down the mortgage on the property, decrease your liabilities, increase your equity, and grow your net worth over time. Using the principles, hacks, and methods of in the following pages, you will be able to multiply your real estate holdings in a short period of time.

Chapter 1 Fundamental of Real Estate Investment

Real Estate Investment Trust (REITs) is an investment trust where a group of people invests their money in residential or commercial real estate business. These trusts use mortgages of large numbers and commercial properties and manage them. Such trusts show both shares and real estate's best features. Invest in real estate investment just the same way an organization operates revenue-generating business assets such as hotels, warehouses, apartments, and shopping centers. While different property types are available, many of these REITs are limited and focus solely on any one type of property. Companies specializing in health care are known as REITs of health care. Such trusts were established in 1960 to allow large-scale investment in the real estate sector, which individual investors can then access. The main advantage of these trusts is that they help people pick a share to invest in a variety of a company rather than investing in a single large estate or house.

Most of these trusts are grouped into three subsections: equity, mortgage, and hybrid. The first class is the property owners and loans are also given to property owners. The second category comprises of ownership and property-generating income management. The mortgage investment trusts are the ones that provide money by acquiring their loans and mortgage-backed securities to property owners.

In several respects, these investment trusts differ significantly from limited partnerships — one of the significant differences is in how their investors disclose the annual tax data.

A company must share 90 percent or more of all its taxable income within its shareholders for a day in the year to become a real estate investment trust. Once the company is eligible as REIT, it can go through its shareholders ' dividends.

Academic concept

Real estate has been defined as land (or immovable assets) along with anything permanently attached to it, such as buildings, and investment is the use of money to purchase property for the sole purpose of income holding or renting. It is fair then to assume (combining both definitions) that investment in immovable property includes the purchase of immovable property (or investment in the immovable property) for income generation, profit-making, and assets acquisition.

The Conceptual Description

Leverage, unlike stock investments (usually requiring more equity from the investor), a real estate investment (heavily) can be leveraged. With an investment in real estate, you can use money from other people to increase the return rate and manage a much more significant investment otherwise not possible.

Investing in real estate tax shelter provides tax advantages. Annual after-tax cash flows, equity buildup through asset appreciation, and cash flow following tax on sale are yields. Non-monetary refunds Investment in real estate provides ownership pride, security in which you monitor ownership, and diversification of portfolios.

Nevertheless, investing in real estate is not a bed of roses. Investment in real estate requires capital, risks exist, and rental property can be intensive in terms of management. The clothes you wear requires money, on the other hand, for a car, it includes risk driving, and it certainly requires management. The difference is that a car is not a wealth source.

How to become an investor

In real estate, develop a goal of investing in real estate. What would you like to do you want to do, and by what time do you want to do it? What rates of return do you expect to earn on money that you squeeze out of your home or bank account to buy an investment property because of the risk?

Know what you need to look for returns and how to measure them. Unless you can read music, you can't succeed in music. Invest in an excellent investment course in real estate or technology for investment in real estate where you can learn how to monitor returns and calculate formulas.

Be vigilant about the schemes of Getting Rich. Many so-called gurus are ready to teach you how to make millions of property investments with real estate. But let logic be your guide; we assume a map is published by no one who discovers a gold mine.

Establish a relationship with a real estate agent who is familiar with the local real estate market and understands rental property. Spending time with the "agent of the year" will not advance your investment goals unless that person knows about investment property and is adequately prepared to help you get it right. Choose a broker who understands investment in real estate.

What Are Real Estate Investment Trusts?

Is there a secret formula for investment in real estate? Looking at property moguls, including Donald Trump, who made millions of investments in real estate, we usually think that investing in real estate needs to have some unique blueprint, but that's not always the case.

There are some fundamentals, golden rules, and unchangeable realities that relate to investment in real estate, whether you're a first-time dabbler or a seasoned professional. Most of these are common sense, only good old-fashioned.

Do Your Homework. At the time, there are plenty of shops to have on the market, as distressed homeowners scuttle to realize their investments, maintain their financial stability, and avoid foreclosure. Still, when faced with a deal that seems too good to be true, it might just be.

Making sure you leave whether substantial changes are intended in the area- a significant industrial development or a new highway extension from your doorstep could limit the profits you will make on your investment in real estate!

Find out how often To Invest. There are several reasons why people like to invest. Do you want a long-term investment that will give you rental income, or are you looking for a property that you can update quickly and sell for a profit? Do you focus on the fickle residential market, or do you prefer a more stable market for commercial real estate?

Understanding what your goals are in structuring and planning your portfolio of investment in real estate is vital for the very first time.

Know Your Risk Appetite. Great reward comes with considerable risk. Occasionally.

Understanding whether you can manage the sometimes challenging high-risk investment climate, in real estate or otherwise, will help guide you in making the right choices. If you don't have the appetite for the pressure which follows it, there's no use opting for a higher risk portfolio of investment properties. If you think higher-risk investments are stressful, they may not be for you!

If you choose safer options, investment in real estate can still work for you, pick a property in developed areas where your rental income and steady growth are more stable.

Maybe don't extend yourself. It is maybe tempting to bite off more than you can chew when you're caught in the high that accompanies successful real estate investment. However, consider that if you invest in renting out your properties, there may be times when you cannot find suitable tenants. Can you cover all your property payments if that happens? If not, reconsider your plans, and proceed accordingly.

Real Estate Investing is a safe choice. Whichever your answers to the questions mentioned above, real estate remains a safe and profitable choice. Understanding your ambitions, personality, or if you are in lengthy-haul real estate investment or a quick buck, will help you make sound choices, give you a balanced portfolio, and make sure your investments pay dividends over the coming years.

WHAT IS TURN-KEY REAL ESTATE INVESTING?

This is a simple concept where the buyer is buying, rehabilitating, and then reselling a property at a profit. This is also referred to as a home, "flipping." The process usually occurs remotely, as the investor resides in her or his own house, sometimes in a place where flipping does not make any sense and uses the Internet to locate and invest in opportunities. The target here is to make the process of investing in real estate as easy as possible, so all the investor has to do is flip a switch or "change the button." Usually, instead, you purchase a minor home that contains a single family, repair it to match current codes, and make sure it attracts the buyers. Below is how its work: the property is purchased by a turnkey retailer or company.

One or more investors buy a share or all of the house's stock. To make it new and attractive to customers, the seller or company "fix-up" or rehabilitates the property.

Once the property has been rehabilitated, it will be put back on the resale market.

Once a sale is completed, the buyer gets his or her money back plus any gain gained, depending on the share of the investment he or she owns.

This could be a sound investment technique if it is done correctly. You have made a benefit from flipping the home as the buyer, and you can have as little or as much interest as you want. You can be as interested in the flipping process as you want, helping to manage the home treatment contractors, and leaving the entire process to the turnkey retailer.

Why not buy and rent a house myself?

You may think you can remove the middleman, the turnkey distributor, or company, and do all the legwork yourself. While this is what many shareholders do and excel in, there are some drawbacks. You will end up doing a lot more work in most situations than you would as an investor.

Here's what you'd have to do if you became a flipper instead of using a turnkey approach and managing the operation for you by the turnkey retailer.

Finding a property: - First, a suitable property would have to be located.

Rehabilitating house:- First, the estate should be restored and rehabilitated, adhering to existing codes and also being an outstanding one-family property. It requires proper budgeting and treatment of contractors and staff, which requires a presence on-site.

Marketing this property for rent or sale: You'd have to look for a paying tenant or a buyer to live in the house once the property is ready to move in.

You'd be entering a whole new dimension when you want to rent the property. Check out our overview of that investment strategy for more details on turnkey real estate investment where you lease rather than resell.

If it sounds like a lot of effort, it's because it is. With turnkey real estate investment, you can take off your hands as much or little of the work and put it on other people. Let us have a glance at the benefits of turnkey investment in real estate. The benefit of turnkey real estate investment is that a turnkey retailer is an investor, not a landlord or a flipper, in a full-fledged turnkey real estate investment scenario. The property should be managed for you, you are employing someone else, and all you have to do is collect on the income. Here are some of the main benefits of turnkey investment in real estate.

It does not need your presence locally. You acquire single-family property in remote locations with turnkey real estate investment. This allows you the freedom to stay where you want while maintaining a cash flow from a location with excellent property values. For example, you could continue to live in the gated community in Texas, where the flipping house may be meaningless while investing in rentable or flippable properties in Seattle or elsewhere that have a strong demand for such properties.

Easy diversification of your turnkey real estate investment portfolio could be a good move while done correctly. One element of successfully implementing a turnkey investment strategy for real estate is appropriately investing in multiple markets, which is easy to do as it takes little to no time of its own. The benefits of investing in various markets are simple: it protects you from an unforeseen economic downturn.

Since turnkey investment in real estate makes it so easy to have multiple properties, if you do it right, this is an essential advantage of the investment strategy. Don't put all your eggs in one basket, in other words.

If working with a reputable turnkey real estate retailer or company, the provider knows the real estate markets much more accurately than an outsider might. You can probably do some basic research on an area, checking out local school scores, crime reports, and price range, but a turnkey company would know all that and more; they'll see the heart of a community.

The disadvantages of turnkey investment in real estate. If turnkey investment in real estate sounds like a sure-fire way of making money, you should be aware that the strategy has disadvantages. First and foremost, you will find turnkey manufacturers trying to maximize their profits at the risk of cutting corners, but there are other pitfalls beyond that.

The "middle man" has to make money. The turnkey business is a business, and it needs to make money for that business. That means buying property at a discount and selling it to you at a higher amount of the property, often for a substantial profit margin. The turnkey company will then be able to make an additional profit by managing the sale or rental of the property for you. Though, one thing to remember about this downside is that turnkey businesses often have a marketing machine going at all times and can find incredible deals in their business, enabling them to give you a lot even as the company makes its money.

There are "shady" turnkey companies out there, and you have to trust someone. Such firms would allow an out-of-state investor to purchase a bad property in a bad location, which means more money going out of the hands of the buyer than flowing in. You have to rely on the experience, skills, and reputation of the turnkey operator to make a good deal for you. This means that you have to deal with someone you truly can trust.

As a result of this, Turn-key real estate investment, has significant benefits, and it can certainly be an enticing practice for cash flow. Nonetheless, disadvantages also need to be taken into account before making any deals. You'll need to research the turnkey provider to make sure they're both reliable and successful and make sure that the cash flow opportunity they're giving you is practical and feasible. Turnkey investment in real estate is a great way to make money as long as you're smart about it and take care of your due diligence throughout the process.

How Does Real Estate Investing Work?

Investing in real estate works best with a strategy. In deciding how you want to invest in real estate to work for you, it is necessary first to determine the results you wish to get from investment in real estate — looking to build wealth, or quick cash, or both? You could choose a brief-term strategy, a lengthy-term strategy, or a mixture of the two, depending on your desired results.

How does it work to make quick cash by investing in real estate?

Quick cash could be developed with a brief-term investment strategy for real estate, including fast turning or flipping property. Fast turning property (buying and selling immediately) can provide substantial and fast cash if you buy correctly. The estate is usually placed under a low price contract and then sold at a higher price to include again. Based on your plan, the property can be sold with or without changes. Quick turn deals can quickly produce between $2K and $30K plus depending on the contract and whether it's a sharp turn for wholesale or retail.

Wholesale Fast Turn

Wholesale fast turns involve finding a product below market value and selling the offer quickly at a wholesale price. You give your buyer, usually another shareholder, the opportunity to make a profit by selling wholesale (below retail). Wholesaling is always a way to make zero, or little, transactions with money down. It is a means for real estate investors to get around the house flipping used for financial support. Let's presume you're seeking a motivated seller, willing to sell your house at $200K. You contract the property with the seller for $200 K and find another buyer who likes the deal and is willing to pay $110K. Your agreement with the seller would then be transferred to your buyer for $20K. In reality, the buyer closes and buys the property from the seller; and a $20K assignment fee is charged to you at the closing. The form used for retail is an alternative. You could place an option on a property and then sell the option again to another shareholder. In reality, you never have to buy the property with assignments and options to make money.

Retail Fast Turn

Short turns involve finding a property well below market value and getting it ready for retail sale. Your target customer is a homeowner rather than an investor with fast shifts in retail. You could buy a property that requires a little effort, a bit of work, or you may not need to do any work at all because you purchased it at a discount from a motivated seller. You market and sell the property at a retail price once the property is ready.

How does it work to build wealth by investing in real estate?

Wealth is created by long-term investment strategies for real estate, the purchase, and keeping of land. The investor purchases a property in this scenario and then rents it to a tenant or leases it to a tenant with the option to purchase it.
Renting
Renting is about finding a house, getting it ready for rent, and marketing it for rent. The investment strategy for rental property offers a number of prospects for profit. If the mortgage is less than monthly rental income and other expenses, cash flow is created. Long-term wealth is created through property appreciation, mortgage payment by tenants, and tax benefits.

Imagine getting ten apartments paid in full for a cash flow of $10,000 and rented for $1,000. If flats are worth only $100K each, you'd have an asset worth $1 million-plus a cash flow of $10 K per month before spending. This financial position can be reached in your timeline reasonably and easily. Some people buy one or two houses a year, while others immediately purchase several homes.

Lease Option

Lease options are provided by providing a lease property with the option to buy (usually for twelve months or more). Including revenue from the initial incentive charge, monthly cash flow from the rent, profit from the sale when the option is exercised, and tax benefits, which are a variety of profit centers with lease options.

Finally, the answer to the question, "How does real estate investment work?" really depends on how you want real estate investment to work for you. Whether you're building wealth, leaving the 9-5, early retirement, quick cash, or financial freedom, you can get it through investment in real estate. Investing in real estate, such as buying at a loss and generating instant equity, creating capital by tenants paying down a loan, appreciation, cash flow, interest, and tax benefits, has numerous benefits. Determine the strategy, lengthy-term, brief-term, or a mixture of the two, and invest in real estate that works for you.

A Beginner's Guide For Real Estate Investor

When selecting your first property to purchase and deciding to enter the current market, real estate investment for beginners involves a few things to consider. For learners, we plan to address some of the concerns that are engaged in this form of investment. You have to understand that by making the wrong decision, most people lose money. Buying while stock prices are low and selling when they are high is the key to making money in real estate. Before you determine on your first property and enter the real estate investment field, we will give you essential tips to think about.

The number one principle of investing in a property is the location- the location is one of the first things to think about. If you think about which property you want to purchase, you need to think about areas that might be anticipated shortly to become popular locations but have prices that have not yet risen. This may indicate that they are situated in the outer parts of the city or that they may be located near a proposed resort area. If you're looking to invest in property, think about whether it's going to be better than some other real estate investment locations.

You may want to consider investing in lower-priced real estate than market prices. You may find the right property offers that an owner needs to sell due to a job transfer or divorce. This may imply you could get the property at cheaper prices than most other homes in the area, and when you sell, you will have better chances of making a profit. You can find a property that needs a few repairs, or needs a paint coat and adding a few minor details. When you start investing in real estate, these can be the best chances to make better profits.

Having land that can be leased out to fund the mortgage payment is another thing to think about. If you're paying the best price and getting the proper funding for property you're buying, then you could rent it till the demand increases, and you can make a profit. Keep in mind that you'll have to find a suitable renter and pre-screen them to find those who pay their bills on time and won't harm your estate. You do not want the additional cost of hiring an attorney and evicting renters who haven't paid rent or caused damage, but it can be part of real estate investment.

If you want a mortgage in which you invest, you must ensure that there is no penalty clause for early payment of the loan. When you buy the property and repair it to sell quickly, this can happen. You could make a profit this way, but when you sell it, you could have a penalty for paying off the loan early. Most banks understand that you are trying to repair and sell the property, but if they know you are investing in real estate, they will require a higher down payment.

Think of ways you can save money when it comes to closing costs and land charges. When you find property for sale by sellers, you can get better deals because they protect the fee for the seller. Such charges may be 7 to 10 percent of the price of the property, but it is a charge that the seller pays. Most buyers are always using agents to help them find the best deals. The critical thing to consider is that when you're investing in real estate, you get the best price on the property and don't charge the market price.

When investing in properties, do not make these common mistakes. When making property offers, think carefully, and don't rely on gut instincts because they're not always right. Before investing in properties, make sure you do your homework and find out as much as you can.

Inspect the properties and consider a professional home inspector for significant defects. Do not depend on rumors or promises in the popularization of a particular region or rising prices due to plans to grow it. Do not be emotionally involved with properties because when you are investing in real estate, it can cause you to make bad decisions that cost money.

When you intend to invest in real estate, you've heard some of the most important things to think about. There may be small things that make a big difference when it comes to making a profit for the beginners in this sector. You need to find out as much as you can about the estate you are involved in and get expert assistance before you enter the field of investment inland. To help you find the best deals and get some professional advice to help you make the best decision, you can contact a local real estate agent. Once you enter the real estate investment market, this should be your next step.

Real Estate Investing - Is it a Wise Investment?

I still find it interesting that you hear so many stories about people who made tons of money in real estate rentals, but never about regular accidents, as people don't talk so much about them. Much as you always learn about the winnings of a gambler, but never the full amount of their losses.

Among the most critical parts of owning a single property is to understand the concepts and see them as a corporation

Here are the main reasons why I don't recommend investing directly in real estate properties:

1) It's one of the few investments that can cost you considerable money and time.

Owning property like an investment include costs like interest on the loan, cost of closing, cost of locating tenants, cost of months without tenants, cost of additional insurance, cost of restoring and maintaining an investment property, and management fees to name a few. Most people don't consider all property ownership costs.

2) It is an asset leveraged to increase the risk.

Whether it's a home, apartment building, or property, most people take out a loan to purchase the investment. Their initial investment is leveraged, and they bet that the investment will be worth more. Gains and losses are magnified by leverage. (This is good on the upside, terrible on the downside.) If the price of the real estate market has plummeted, you may not be able to sell the property for what you put in, and you still have a monthly cash outflow obligation.

3) The portfolio is not diversified.

Some real estate is an investment in a particular location of one house. In this one basket, you usually put many of your eggs, which again increases the risk. (Diversification is among the most critical priority tenants. I am a fan of low-cost mutual funds and ETFs because of g on the real estate market. Even in good markets, selling and closing on a property usually takes more than two months. Anyone who owned a home during a buyer's market, like now, can tell you their nightmare and frustration over a year (or years) with the house on the market. How about a holiday home?

Even when it comes to holiday homes, if you want to use a holiday home as your holiday home, do it if it makes financial sense to you. I see that as a little investment other than just buying a second home. The satisfaction and happiness you get from having a holiday home make up for the real estate's risks and costs. A vacation home's main objective is to be used and enjoyed differently from a property purchased primarily as an investment. (Often, renting a holiday home for several weeks a year is much cheaper and more convenient than getting the cost of owning a holiday home.) REITs- whether you believe in it and want to invest in real estate, I am a fan of real estate investment trusts or REITs. REITs are security that trades like a stock and invests directly in real estate through the ownership of a portfolio of properties and mortgages.

1) Having an expert picking up assets

2) Without the hassle, costs and responsibility to manage an individual property

3) Not incurring the risk of personal property due to lack of diversification (because the REIT may purchase many properties, mortgages and/or locations)

4) It is marketable.

5) A REIT alone is a diversified investment conclusion. Although I do not suggest buying individual real estate as an investment, real estate as an asset class usually improves the diversification of your portfolio as it has a low correlation with the general market. Therefore, I generally recommend that you devote a small portion of your portfolio to this category, not as a market call to this sector (especially now), but based on my confidence in its potential to dampen your portfolio's overall long-term volatility.

Please note that because we are not great fans of REITs right now, mainly commercial property REITs, we must be in the potential as the economy is improving and less demand due to lower prices.

Chapter 2 What To Expect In The Real Estate Business

Starting a real estate business is a daunting task. It may not be that easy looking at those who have made it in the area and concluding it's a walk in the park. It takes a lot of hard work, good decision making, patience, tolerance, and learning. If you are ready to pick lines from the gurus in the area, you will find running a real estate an easy task. However, you may need to be more determined to get your business up by investing everything in it. For most of the people in the industry, they have experienced hardships in the first year of starting the business, and those who are brave make it higher.

Getting into the real estate business does not need you to expect more than you can offer. You need to concentrate on building it fast than thinking about the profits and how you will handle it. Rather start by learning ways on how to make it better and grow. You need not get distracted on the way as that may lead to your failure early in the business. Make sacrifices and ensure you have gained what it takes to be the best in the industry. It is not easy at first, but once you get used to it, you will grow to love it.

The real estate business is an interesting industry as you get to meet different people, locations, buildings, and so on. You first need to love it to do it. If you keep the mentality that you can do it without loving it, then this is not for you. It's also not for the fainted hearted as it requires a lot of work and sacrifices to pick up.

What is the real estate business all about?

Before going into the industry, you need to be well versed in what you are dealing with. You should understand all the aspects of real estate and how it works.

Real estate is considered as a property that includes land, buildings, natural resources, crops, roads, and other immovable things. It can also be the professional act of selling, renting, and buying land and generally houses. It also deals with human activity that is involved in making improvements to the land. On the other hand, real property deals with the rights that a property has. For instance, the interests that come from human activities.

Why choose the real estate business?

The real estate business is a fast-growing investment strategy that takes more than hard work. You need to be dedicated and sacrifices to make sure your needs are met. However, they may be affected by market changes or conflict, and you need to have knowledge of what type of real estate business you need to venture into. It is so interesting working on something you love and feel safe handling. It is always hard at first but can turn out to be the best over time.

Making a decision to embark on the real estate business takes a lot of courage and commitment. However hard it may be at the beginning, there is always a greater reward in the future. Here are the reasons as to why you have to consider real estate business:

It is so easy to get in

Unlike other professionals who take a longer time to get employment or while studying, the real estate industry does not require a lot of skills to become one. You can be a real estate agent with a limited number of skills or knowledge and learn more on the way. Once you get in, you will easily fit in. In most firms, there are a number of part-time workers or students too. It's easier to learn and adapt. The knowledge you seek is always within your reach. For example, you can acquire it from the realtors or your mentors.

There is an easier profit-making

Starting out on your business may not be that simple. However, once you have mastered how to grow your business and know how to get more clients to buy the real estate you are selling, you will automatically feel a boost in your bank. It is a lucrative industry, and working hard for profits is essential. Once you work hard, you are sure to get something in return at all times.

You will more likely work hard
As much as it is easy to work hard for your business, you may need to have a form of appreciation for what you do. You should feel and experience the results of your hard work in a unique way. The more the hard work, dedication, and determination, the easier it is to receive positive results.

It is interesting

You will not have that life of a professional who always sits in an office from Monday to Monday, getting bored and feeling like quitting all the time. There are a number of trends that change, markets, and the environment. You will most likely be at the field or place of construction to see if it's taking the right direction and so on. You may even interact with people who see life from a different perspective, and sharing experiences will make it even more worthwhile.

Types of real estate businesses

There are six types of real estate types for you to choose from. Once you select the one you need, you should not be distracted to do all of them at once. It will be better to concentrate and give your all to one that really fits your needs and interest. However, some investors have invested in different types of real estate business to make more profit. As it is, what works for you may not work for someone else.

You should ensure you do a thorough research analysis to determine the possibility of making a profit or a loss. Choosing the right type will sorely depend on your needs, goals, circumstances, and market. Getting the perfect location for all your construction needs is very important. This is because it will determine whether your business will pick up or not. Choosing the type that fits you requires you be ready to invest in a kind of property while knowing the risks involved and the amount of involvement needed. Making the right investment will guarantee your profits. Read and understand what you need and how to go about it. These include the following:

1. Raw Land

This consists of undeveloped land, ranches, and working farms. It mostly includes everything on land, which is trees and water. It can also consist of air rights, minerals, and other natural resources, for example, oil and metals. It also includes agricultural practices. Land can be used in a number of ways, from construction to farming. Choosing the right land for all your needs may not be that easy, but through research and extensive reading, you will have an idea of what is needed for that particular real estate investment. You should consider looking for a location that will attract further investors when it comes to selling the land or property. It is on-demand nowadays as it will give you the opportunity to construct something you have always looked forward to from scratch.

2. Residential real estate

Mostly fall under the category of single-family homes, townhouses, condominiums, duplexes, triple-deckers, and high-value homes. They mostly deal with houses or sites of construction as well as selling and resale of houses. It is among the most popular investment in real estate that yields maximum profits. However, for any residential real estate investments, you need to have another plan as it tends to be affected by markets. Once the market is affected, there will have a small number of investors. What you can use is the wholesaling, buy and hold and also rehabbing strategies to survive the bad business days.

3. Industrial real estate

This mostly consists of warehouses, industries, factories, power plants, and other manufacturing buildings. Most of these buildings are preferred for distribution of goods and services, production, research as well as storage. These buildings tend to be different from other kinds; thus, the zone is to be selected carefully, so is the construction. For these kinds of buildings, you should mostly consider an environment that is a distance away from residential homes, as that may have an effect on their health. It should be in an open property for more air circulation and less pollution. The location to be considered should be ideal for producing goods in the most effective way without having to pollute the environment and destroy property.

4. Commercial real estate

These, on the other hand, are considered commercial as they are used to produce income. They include shopping malls, educational institutions, hospitals, and hotels, strip malls, parking facilities, stores, entertainment facilities, and office space. In most cases, most of them are used for businesses rather than residences. They also require very little management.

5. Special purpose real estate

This kind of property is set aside for special purposes such as schools, cemetery, and places of worship, government buildings, parks, and libraries. Most of these places cannot be owned by a single person. Most properties of this kind are strategically constructed to meet the needs of the investors. You may find that it does not take a lot of time in construction. As long as the property is unique, it can easily attract the interested party.

6. Mixed-use

In this area, this type of real estate property deals with incorporating types. In this case, you can have the residential and industrial together or any other two. For example, you can have a mall and a warehouse on the same property. This needs you to have enough knowledge and the ideal location for your business. Not all of them can work together or be convenient at the same place. You need to be careful of your choices, as that may affect your investment in the future. Let's say, for instance, you construct a factory and a hospital on a piece of land. That will not work effectively as the factory will be emitting poisonous gases into the air while the hospital takes care of the sick people and help them get better. Most factory gases are hazardous to the environment, humans, and animals.

What you should expect in the real estate business

Most people make a mistake of expecting everything to turn out easy as they may have thought. This is not the case with real estate businesses. They are faced with a lot of competition, and you need to keep your business up to be the best. You need to invest in your business and strive to make it unique as much as possible to remain relevant. If you are willing to learn and sacrifice, you will surely get the deserving results.

Here is what you need to keep in mind when starting your business:

Not an easy task

Starting the real estate business may not be that rosy at first, as it will take a toll on your time and sleep, thinking about the best ways to grow and improve your businesses. You may need to research a lot on the market, the location of the property as well as the gents you will use to get clients, and so on. To ensure everything is going on smoothly, it will take a lot of hard work, determination, and sacrifice. Success and profits will not come on easily. It takes time and perseverance. You should not be faint-hearted if you need to experience success. Always keep in mind the idea that you have crossed the battle line, and you have to do everything it takes to emerge the winner.

Be creative

For any real estate business, you should expect to be more open to ideas. Learning new things and how well to solve the challenges in the real world will help you grow your business. As much as you have the knowledge and expertise in your profession, it will take more than that to come up with the right decision to help you grow. You do not have to rely on your family and friends to help you solve your work issues. Being your own boss comes with a lot of responsibilities that need you to be reliable and go beyond your comfort zone to see you grow into a successful real estate agent. You will learn how to handle your issues peacefully within yourself and use the most innovative and creative ideas to help your business improve and make the decisions right for it.

You will need help

When starting out your business, you are probably afraid of getting new experiences. At the same time, you may find yourself excited about seeing your business grow. As you may be new in the industry, you may need somewhere to lay your shoulder on. You may have to ask for help with running your business. Most real estate agents use brokers (salespeople who have expertise and experience in negotiating deals). They are a great resource for the growth of your business. They will prepare you for what you will meet on the way to your success and how you need to finalize deals or decide on the property value as they have been on the market for long. They work on a commission, and they navigate the market easily to get you potential customers. Where you are not well versed, you should feel free to ask those who have experience in the industry. Who knows, you may learn a thing or two on how to improve your business. Before gaining more knowledge and experience, you will pass through challenges that will require you to make the right decision for your team or business. Listening to other people's experiences would help you make it right.

Make room for disappointments

Like any other business out there, you need to make room for failures. It may not be that easy to be relevant in the industry within a day. It takes a lot of time and effort to become somebody. You may feel like giving up at some point in the journey, but reminding yourself why you chose to start it in the first place may help you remain firm. You will, at some point, be disappointed by your team or the tenants you sold or rented a house to. In most situations, the tenants are always hard to handle and want to control you, but getting good ones takes a miracle. Always be prepared for disappointments will save you from heartbreak all the time as you had already prepared your mind of failures once something negative comes about. By easily accepting mistakes and learning from them will greatly help. You can learn to take things easy next time. It's simple and effective once you plan for its possibility. Choosing to ignore and handling issues amicably should keep you going. You can strive to make yourself better.

Profits

Real estate businesses are very popular with successful profits. Once you have mastered the art of convincing your potential clients into buyers, you may have to sit and wait for your bank alert. It takes a lot of time and patience, but once you have a perfect property most people are yearning for, you will easily sell them. You need to research more on the kind of location that mostly fits a particular type of real estate business and strive to get properties of the best quality. Not overpricing will definitely get you more clients. As small the profits may be at first, you can invest them in a more meaningful way to help secure your future and save you during tax payment. It is a lucrative business, and it really reaps benefits.

You need to grow your business

Once you start a business, you need to look for ways to make it grow. Consider using your knowledge, expertise, and influence to grow the leads and networks. You need to build relationships with people. The more people know you, the more there will be potential buyers. It may not be an easy task, but you need to market yourself. Let people know what you are selling or what you are into. Putting yourself out there will greatly help you make the right networks. You can simply connect with your family and friends, attend community gatherings, and use online platforms for marketing you as a brand. However, it may not be simple as you need to sacrifice a lot to get what you are looking for.

Stick to your plan and budget

This is an important part of the real estate rule. Once you make plans on how to run the business, you should not mostly dwell on how to get clients while forgetting what you need to do to make a great impression on your business. That being said, your budget should not exceed your ability. You should not forget your needs and invest everything you have in the business. Ensure you have a budget that covers all the areas of your life, not leaving anything behind and sticking to the budget. The more times you add money to the already formed budget, there is a possibility you will have a shortage in other areas. Be disciplined when handling money and not forgetting you and your business needs as well. A good plan will always yield good results. Always being prepared will help a great deal.

You need a license

For you to become a qualified real estate agent, you need to be a qualified broker for you to open your own business. There is a broker exam that takes up to months to complete or work under a broker to gain knowledge on selling a property. Brokers are highly experienced in the business as they help get potential clients and getting commissions in return. For different states, there are varying broker tests that should be done to make you an experienced real estate agent.

Chapter 3 Choosing the Best Location for Your Real Estate Investment

We have all heard the expression "Location! Location! Location!" when it comes to real estate investing. From simply buying a family home to purchasing a multimillion-dollar investment property, the experts all agree, the number one determiner of if you have a sound investment is, you guessed it, location. But what exactly is a prime real estate location? Can you still make money while buying in prime locations? Can you make money by using a different model, buying in sub-prime locations? In this chapter, we will attempt to answer these questions and many more.

Why is location so essential in real estate?

"Location! Location! Location!" the cardinal rule that is preached by every real estate agent and investor. So many things factor into the decision to buy real estate and where to buy it. Why is location the most important consideration when buying?

The truth is the biggest importance to location is that it is the one thing about a property that you cannot change. You buy a house that has horrible orange shag carpeting from the 1970's. That's not a big deal. Laying down new flooring is an easy and relatively inexpensive fix. But if you buy a house next to a busy airport, major highway and that has railroad tracks that have trains running all day and night. Those are things that you can't fix. It can be a luxury mansion with all the upgrades, but you still can't change the fact that there is a cacophony of trains, planes, and automobiles all day and all night. Obviously, this is an extreme example (though I did see a property like this once), but the principle is true. You can change a lot of things about a property, but you cannot change the location. Therefore, location is one of the most important factors to consider when buying a new property. But how do we determine if a location is a good location or a bad location?

Factors that Determine a Locations Value

There are many factors that are used to determine if a property has good or bad value. Sometimes those factors aren't as cut and dry as you would imagine. Sometimes what you consider good or bad depends upon your investment strategy. In this chapter, we will first look at things that traditionally make a property a good investment. Then we will explore what makes a property a good investment for some less traditional investment strategies.

Neighborhood

Before buying a property, drive around the area. Look at the condition of the other properties in the neighborhood. This is particularly important when investing in residential real estate. Are the homes generally well maintained? Are there a significant number of vacant lots or vacant properties? Talk to people who live in the area. Are the police often called to this neighborhood? Do people generally stay for at least five years once they buy? Or are properties a revolving door of buyers and sellers? You can learn much about an area simply by asking questions and listening to the residents of the area.

You can also find out good information by visiting the local library. They usually have reference materials and statistics on local neighborhoods.

Wealth

It is good to look at an area that has some degree of wealth. Having a wealthy "part of town" for lack of a better term, is important because it having wealth in the area helps to offset any overall turn down in the economy For example, if there is an economic downturn in manufacturing, the wealth of the area will ensure that much of the retail and restaurant business remain viable, protecting the overall real estate value of the area.

Job Market

If an area has a strong job market, people are going to want to live there. It's as simple as that. Jobs increase the value of properties in an area. For example: In 2018 a major car manufacturer moved its US corporate headquarters and some manufacturing to Plano, Texas. For six months before their opening and for a year after their opening the housing values for homes for a 45-mile radius around the newly opened offices increased by an average of 20%. New jobs meant the need for more housing. More people in the area brought more restaurants and shopping in some of the smaller towns. These long-term improvements to the towns increased their property values for a much longer time. They became more enticing to new home buyers as places to live.

Attractions and Convivences

People like to live where there are things to do for entertainment, convenient shopping, transportation, and public services. It the area you are looking at has these things, your property will keep its investment value. Look around the area. Is there a choice of restaurants, convenient grocery and clothing stores? Are there easily accessible medical facilities? Are there fun things to do: movie theaters, restaurants, bars, sports arenas, or concert venues? All of these will increase the value of your investment property and the value of the area that they are in.

Crime Rates

It is important to know the crime rates and statistics of the area that you are looking to invest in. People are looking to live where they feel they and their families will be safe. It is logical really. If you find an area where there has been a string of house robberies in the past months, the housing values will suffer. If the neighborhood is a known gang area or known to have drug houses, this will affect the value of your property and the chances of finding good renters for it (if you are going the rental route of investment).

Neighborhood Future Prospects

This factor is a bit more difficult to quantify. This is where experience and a good gut instinct come into real estate investment. You can buy a house in one of the best neighborhoods in the area, but if that neighborhood is on the decline, your property will lose value over time. However, you can buy a property in an area that is not in the best neighborhood, but if that neighborhood is up and coming, your investment will continue to increase in value. As a beginning investor, this is a hard call to make. But there are some practical things for you to look at that can help when making this call.

•   Research the housing prices over the last ten years. Is the overall trend increasing or decreasing property sale prices? It is important that you look at the overall trend over the ten years and not focus on "micro" upturns or downturns in the market.

•   Look at the overall business trends over the last ten years. Are there more business opening or closing? How long does a new business stay open in general? You want to see the business opening and staying open as an overall trend.

•   What is the average time a property stays on the market? In a strong market, the properties don't last long when they are put up for sale.

•   What is the vacancy rate of the area? If there is a high vacancy rate, there is a likelihood that your property will sit empty for a while. This is an investment killer when in the rental investment business. Also, rising vacancy rates show that people are leaving the area, not moving in. This is a good indicator of a declining market.

"Find out where the people are going and buy the land before they get there." -William Penn Adair

Vacant Lots, Lots of Open Land

If you are looking at buying an investment property and there is a lot of open land of vacant lots available for building, keep in mind that you will have more competition in the future. This isn't necessarily a deal killer as new construction is the sign of a growing economy. However, it is important to remember that all that new construction means that, soon, you will have a lot more properties competing for the same renters and buyers. You can check with the town or county to determine how many new construction permits have been issued and the forecasted population growth. This will give you a better idea of what factors you will be contending with from the new construction arena.

If you are a beginning real estate investor, I encourage you to look at properties in several diverse areas and then compare these facts on each property. This will give you a good idea of where your first property should be bought. For a first or second investment property, I encourage investors to be more conservative in their approach towards buying properties. It is good to have a couple of steady earners in your portfolio before investing in more risky ventures. For your convenience, I have put together a table where you can see all this information at a glance.

Location Facts

Neighborhood   Crime Rate

Job Market   Neighborhood Forecast

Wealth   Available Land

Attractions/ Conveniences New Construction

Non-Traditional Investment Strategies and Location

There are some investment strategies that rely on different location factors or put more emphasis on one of the above factors more than the others. Although I do not necessarily recommend these strategies for new investors, I would be remiss if I did not mention them.

Investing in an "up-and-coming" neighborhood There are many investors that focus their investment strategy on predicting where the growth is going to happen, rather than in already established areas. This is a risky strategy because if you forecast the growth of an area incorrectly, you will get stuck with low-value properties that you will have trouble unloading at the best. Or a worse scenario is that you invest a lot of money into property renovation only to end up upside down on the property and unable to sell it except at a huge loss. However, when this strategy works the profits can be massive. This is the draw of this strategy to investors.

You buy properties in a low value or formerly industrial area at rock bottom prices, put money into renovating them, and then sell them (or rent them out) at a large profit as the property values increase. This strategy is part science, part experience, and part good luck. If, as a new investor, you are looking to invest this way. I cannot stress enough the importance of talking to more experienced investors and getting their thoughts. I encourage new investors to find a mentor who is an investor that is where they would like to be in ten years. This is an area in which such a mentor would be important. You can also research the town and city plans for the area. Is there a large company coming to the area that will push up the demand for properties? Has the city started an improvement initiative in the area that will bring new businesses and city resources to the area? Is the city changing the zoning ordinances from industrial to residential? All these are good indicators that an area will be an "up-and-coming" neighborhood and a good prospect to make money. However, remember, there are no guarantees. More than one investor has lost his or her shirt using this strategy.

Flipping Houses

This is related to the above investment strategy but not quite the same. When flipping houses, you look for homes that are in need of renovation and repair, put the work into doing that renovation, and then sell them for a profit. The best houses for flipping are the ugly duckling houses on the block in prime location areas. The risk in this investment is that you will spend too much on the renovation and will not make a profit. Another risk is that you bite off a project that is more involved than you have the time or ability to handle, and you lose steam partway through the project, having to sell the property for cost or a loss. However, one strategy when flipping houses is buying ugly duckling houses in "up-and-coming" areas. The risks to that are the same as both investing in "up-and-coming" neighborhoods and the risks inherent with flipping houses.

Here are some tips for flipping houses.

- Hire a qualified contractor to assess the renovations needed before buying the property

- Be sure you have the necessary skills to do the renovations or the money to hire professionals to do the things that you do not have the skills in

- Research the building codes and the process for getting building permits in the area that you are looking to buy property in before you purchase the property

- Do not underestimate the time commitment that this project will take from you. Be prepared to say goodbye to your nights and weekends until the project is completed.

"Location! Location! Location!" has been the mantra of real estate agents and investors for good reason. Getting the right location for your investment strategy will bring you one giant step closer to realizing your real estate investment dreams.

Chapter 4 Getting the Right Property to Sell

Now that you have got into the business of real estate wholesaling, the next vital step you need to make is to get the right property. Remember that the property you get is what will determine the amount of profit that you make at the end of it al.

While this is the simplest method for you to make much money in the real estate market, it also presents you with a challenge because you need to have the best property for wholesale. We have different tactics and levels of flipping houses this way, including the different types of properties that can be wholesaled.

As a real estate wholesaler, you have various options when you decide to sell houses on wholesale. Here are a few options to choose from.

Single Family Homes

This is most probably the most popular type of house for wholesalers. Here are a few reasons that make these houses the best for wholesale purposes:

The prices of these houses usually appreciate faster than multi homes, and they also have a higher rental rate which means that you will attract investors much easily.

These houses are usually cheaper than other types of units that you will opt for. They are therefore lighter on the market and ideal for people that are just getting into the rental business. They will allow you to have more disposable income that you will get to spend on other things.

These houses are relatively easy to maintain and manage, especially when you compare them to multi-apartment buildings. Tenants that are in the houses tend to take them as their own, and this means you won't have to spend a lot of money on renovations. As a property owner, you have an easy time looking at the tenants because they aren't so many like in multifamily apartments.

These rental properties bring in higher rental prices as opposed to every unit in a multi-unit facility. The tenants in these homes enjoy many advantages that will make them be able to pay the high amount that you ask. So, while waiting to flip the house, you can as well make some more money from them.

These houses have a specific tenant base that isn't interested in living in apartment units. The appeal of these houses is in their privacy and the freedom to make use of the garden areas the way someone pleases. You are targeting a market segment that is the biggest – people that are after their own privacy and that need space. This means that the demand for these houses usually remains steady the whole year-round.

These houses are easier to finance compared to other homes. This means you can get a loan for buying the home faster than you can get one for multi-apartment homes. The loans also have a lower interest rate compared to other homes.

Condos and Townhomes

The benefits of buying condos are definitely dependent on what you plan to do with the condo or the townhome. Now that you plan to sell it after a short period let us look at the various benefits that you gain when you invest in condos for wholesaling:

Cash flow – when you buy a condo, you will enjoy some income as you look for a buyer to flip the property. The aim of buying a condo is to try and sell it off in the shortest time possible. But while you wait for this time to reach, you will benefit from the cash flow, which represents the difference between what comes in and what goes out. Additionally, the rents on condos are high, which means you will recoup a small portion of your investment as you wait for the property to sell. The condos appreciate in value, and this means you will be able to profit in the form of passive income. The growth in value is a good way to make more profit compared to letting the property sit and wait.

If you hold onto the condo for some time, you will be able to pay off your loan in the shortest time possible. This is because the property will give you the income that you can use.

While you hold onto the property, you will be able to decrease your tax obligations to a large extent. You will be able to write off a portion of your tax obligations.

While waiting for the property to get a market, you will benefit from the passive income that comes with the entail income from tenants. With the help of a property manager, you won't have to do anything – just sit and wait for your income to grow.

As urbanization increase, the condos and townhouses are in very high demand. This is also due to the fact that Millenials and the younger generations love the city and they are attracted to these types of homes.

The demand for these homes is very high, which means that you will sell them off faster and make your profit more easily.

Mobile Homes

Though commonly overlooked, these homes can be as profitable as the other homes that you flip on the market. Let us look at the reasons why mobile homes are ideal for wholesaling purposes:

Compared to single-family houses and multifamily properties, the cost of these mobile homes is lower. This means you can acquire more units at a lower cost.

Since the mobile homeowners are responsible for the repair and maintenance of the homes, and you will not have a lot of work when it comes to renovating the home for sale.

Since you are buying a set of units, you get to spread the risks out, and the risk for losses reduces significantly.

With the demand for these homes hitting all new highs, the need for mobile homes has also increased in equal measure. This means that you will be able to sell off the homes faster than ever. People are now opting for more affordable housing, which means you will be able to sell the house off faster than if you had a different unit.

Not many people have learned the secret of investing in mobile homes, which means that the competition will remain low. You won't have to fight for the available units.

Apartment Buildings

Apartment buildings are some of the top investments for real estate investors. They are usually on demand even if the economy isn't going their way. Here are a few reasons why you need to invest in apartment buildings:

Before you sell it off, you will be able to enjoy a steady source of income. However, you need to choose the apartment in a good area and location, and you will be assured of a steady source of income.

These types of buildings usually provide an affordable housing option that will allow people to enjoy affordable housing, something that they are all after. Apartments will always remain on-demand at all times.

The property can easily appreciate without investing in the property at all. You don't have to invest in new carpets, windows or sidings and paint.

These apartment buildings provide you with tax benefits. One, you will enjoy depreciation expense when you purchase the property, and you can reinvest the proceeds into a new property, and you won't pay any taxes due to the appreciation. The demand for multifamily houses is steady and doesn't experience the dramatic changes that we see in office and retail.

You have access to a host of multifamily loan products that you can choose from to finance the purchase.

Commercial Real Estate

You can also wholesale, retail malls, office buildings, and other mixed-use properties. Here are a few reasons why commercial real estate is an attractive investment for you:

While you wait for your investments to generate interest in the market, you will be able to enjoy the cash returns that come from using the property for rental purposes.

Commercial real estate doesn't fluctuate in the price as compared to other types of investments in the market such as stock and more.

Commercial real estate is less volatile compared to other types of properties. They remain valuable even when the prices rise in the market. This helps to protect you against inflation.

The property enjoys a steady level of appreciation compared to other properties on the market.

When you invest in real estate with the aim of flipping it, you are able to diversify your portfolio the right way.

Vacant Lots and Land

You can sell these vacant lots and land fast because many people are looking to develop their own properties the right way. Here are a few reasons why you can invest in land as a way to make some more money:

When you have a vacant lot, you don't have to do anything on this property at all. It appreciates without investing more money in it.

You don't have to deal with stubborn tenants, leaky roofs, burst pipes, or broken furnaces when you handle the land. Once you buy it, all you need to do is to wait for the land to appreciate.

As a wholesaler of vacant lots, you have little competition to deal with in the first place. Everyone is investing in rental properties, but when you decide to invest in land, you are one among many other people to do this.

When you learn to research and find the right property to sell, you will be able to buy and sell the land without having to see the land yourself. You can make the purchase and sale of the land virtually without leaving home at all.

How to Find Properties for Wholesale Real Estate Investment

Now that you know the kinds of properties that are available for you to invest in, the next step is for you to locate these properties. Remember that you need to find properties that you will sell then make a profit. Here are the top ways to get the property that will make you a hero in wholesaling.

Foreclosure Listings

For you to get the property to sell, you can explore foreclosure listings online. When you decide to go for foreclosure listings, you will be able to achieve a fast purchase, which will give you a better profit compared to others. You, however, will have to do repairs on the property. The good thing is that you will be able to know the price of the property as well as the history, which makes it easy for you to estimate what is required before you put it on the market.

When you buy a foreclosure listing, you have the ability to do all the standard inspections, including research of the title during that period.

When using a foreclosure site, you will only be able to see late-stage foreclosure, which means that you miss out on properties that are in pre-foreclosure, which is the stage where the borrower has already defaulted on the mortgage, but the bank hasn't officially performed the foreclosure.

Property Auctions

Another good place that you can get distressed properties for wholesale auctions. We have various auction sites online that you can use to get the property that you need. You can also check your local newspaper for planned auctions.

If you wish to get more options, you can go for other auction sites that are out of your target area. Many of the auction sites are always updated to give you the latest on the properties that are available.

The good thing is these sites allow you to bid on properties so that you can post the best price you need the property for. Just like other auction sites, they also have a buy it now an option for a few properties.

The competitive bidding process is fast and gives you a chance to bid on houses that you would normally fail to find at a better price. Auctions require you to put down a deposit, usually between 5 and 10 percent and then the remainder in 30-45 days that is if you win the auction.

You can opt for financing from a series of companies that offer to finance specifically for borrowers. These financiers can prequalify you in a few minutes so that you can compete with all-cash buyers.

Real estate auctions will give you a wide range of properties at different price points and will include things such as multi-family units, single homes, as well as commercial properties. Auctions can be online or in person.

These auctions happen in real-time or over a few weeks, and they usually start with a minimum price. From here, the auctioneer will allow the competitive bidder to put up a price for the property until a single person remains. When the auctioneer realizes the price, they will close the auction and then award the property to the winning bidder.

The objective and the investment timeline that you have will dictate what financing options that you have available for you. Cash is the preferred method of payment for the auction. However, you can use lenders to finance the process of paying for the property.

When you get into an auction, you need to budget for the following costs:

Down payment of between 20-35 percent depending on the purchase price of the property as well as any other lender fees.

Holding costs, which are monthly costs that will help, keep the property such as taxes, mortgage, and insurance.

Repair and renovation costs, which vary according to the condition of the property as well as the area.

Marketing costs, which is the amount that you need to spend to put the property on the market. This is usually a percentage of the property and is paid out on the sale proceeds.

Where to Find Auction listings

There are various ways to get real estate auction listings:

Real Estate Auction Sites

You can visit real estate auction sites that offer both online and physical auctions. Some of them offer both types of auctions, while others only offer a single type. You need to check out these sites and browse what they have on offer, they r requirements and more, then start looking for houses that you can bid on.

Real estate Professionals

These have a lot of information regarding upcoming auctions for real estate properties. They include brokers, real estate agents, and trustees. Bankruptcy accountants and lawyers are also good people to engage when you are looking for such opportunities.

You can find these professionals through referrals from friends, investors, and other family members. You can also decide to join a real estate investment group in the area or search for a real estate agent and ask for personal auctions.

Real Estate Classifieds

These are somewhat outdated, but you will still find listings in local newspapers. Some of the newspapers have an online presence as well, and you can get your properties on them.

Abandoned Houses

Another strategy that you can use to get the right property for wholesaling is to go for an abandoned house. An abandoned house is one that no person is living in, and the signs will tell you that the house has been abandoned for a long time. The owners will be paying annual taxes as well as mortgage payments, and so they will be interested in letting it go. You can approach the homeowner directly and make an offer to purchase the home.

If you don't have the time to move around looking for such property, you can go ahead and visit sites that list these properties in the community. These platforms have a search platform that allows you to choose the property type, kind of ownership, and attributes. Most listings come with a phone number attached.

Drive-bys

You can also locate a property for wholesale by moving around the neighborhoods in which you wish to purchase the distressed property. If you see a house that has mail accumulating with the landscaping neglected, it is highly likely that it is abandoned. The house could also belong to a child of a homeowner that is deceased or has gone into a senior facility.

However, you need to approach the home with a lot of caution, because these kids might have an attachment to the home, or they cannot agree to the terms of sale of the property. They might also be avoiding the costly repairs that come with owning such a home and will want to dispose of it. Offering to buy the property will seem to them as an attractive option that they will take up willingly.

While moving around, don't forget to contact the local people that have information on homes that are vacant. These can be mail carriers or real estate agents. Remember that real estate agents will find these homes to be a liability because their clients never want to stay near such homes.

Pre-foreclosures

These are homes where the borrower has defaulted on payment, and they have gone at least for 90 days without paying. Though the agents have in place a process that will help the owner to pay the mortgage, in most cases the property usually goes to foreclosure just because the homeowner cannot afford the amount needed to redeem them.

When you identify a property that is in this state, you get to eliminate most of the competition, and thus you stand a better chance of getting the property. You also have the advantage of negotiating directly with the lender or the borrower while you still have a lot of options on the table.

Attorneys

You will be surprised that you might find a good property from your attorney. Many attorneys run the wills of their clients, and they know when the property is to be sold or not. They also handle divorce settlements, and they know when a couple is undergoing a foreclosure at the close of the divorce, so they will know when a property is on the market or not.

Chapter 5 Common Mistakes to Avoid In Real Estate Investing

Each retail investor dreams of beginning a real estate investment business, making money, and enjoying the "good life." What so many fail to realize is that investing in real estate can be incredibly complicated and expensive if you don't know what you're doing. When you take it slowly and know how to do it properly, it can be very lucrative to invest in real estate. I'll clarify eight common mistakes in this chapter that a new investor typically makes and how to prevent them.

Mistake #1 - Failure to Invest in Education
Attempt to invest in infrastructure before you start paying your rent, and you need to take time to learn the fundamentals of investing in real estate. It does not mean that you need to spend thousands on training or courses related to "guru;" it means that you have to spend time researching the various investment strategies to understand what you need to do to succeed.

Mistake #2-Failure to set up a business. Several people begin investing with their cash, name, and credit on a small scale. What they cannot know is that any mistake could cost you all you've worked so hard to make. Use your homework and produce a business entity that best suits your needs before you start investing. In most instances, the most appropriate company to use for your corporation will be an LLC or a Company. In creating a business company, if something goes wrong down the road, you can cover your assets.

Mistake #3 —Depending on the type of assets you own, and what you plan to do with the property, the type of coverage you will need will be decided. If you're planning to buy a single-family home for sale, you'll need to get a rental agreement. If you are planning to buy and sell "Flip" property, a General Commercial Cost Plan may be the way to go as many will cover the cost of the deal. For best practice, make sure that when determining which type of insurance you will need, you talk to a professional insurance agent.

Mistakes#4 - Failure to Strategize & Plan

Real Estate Investing is like any other company, so why don't you treat it like one? You need to build a clear plan of action on how you will proceed if you want to be successful. Decide which strategy(s) works best for you before you start investing. Don't panic if it takes a while to determine the right plan, but make sure that you stick with it when you find it out.

Mistakes#5- Failure to find and manage a budget

One of the first things you need to do is find out how much cash you need to spend. If you only have enough money for a condo, don't try to buy an apartment complex. Once you've worked out how much money you've got to spend, concentrate your time and energy on a budget that fits your needs. If you're over-budgeting, your growth potential may be reduced. If you're under budget, you're most likely going to get into trouble, resulting in a large amount of debt.

Mistake #6 - Failure to Correctly Estimate the Cost of Repairs

Not only will this mistake cost you time, but it can also cost you the whole deal. Invest in a local contractor to inspect the property to provide you with a list of improvements that will be required and the cost of completing every repair if you are looking to purchase a house. This move will save you time on the back end and thousands of dollars.

Mistake #7 — Failure to create a team. Everyone heard the saying, "You're just as good as the weakest link." If you're trying to invest in real estate and you don't have a strong team behind you, you're going to be the weakest link. It is essential to surround yourself with a great group of people and to continue to have an excellent working relationship with these people. Developing your team can take a lot of time and energy, but when you're finished, demonstrate your progress.

Mistake #8- Failure to take action. After educating yourself, starting a business, securing insurance, defining a strategy or project, developing a budget, and establishing your team, there is nothing left but to put everything to work and take action. At first, it might be daunting. You might make little mistakes, but if you don't take action, you're never going to make money and be successful.

It can be challenging to invest in real estate, and if you go wrong, it can be costly. Investing in real estate, on the other hand, can be very professional and financially beneficial. Don't be afraid to ask a specialist for assistance. If you know what you're doing, most of these errors can be prevented. The more information you acquire and research, the fewer errors you make.

Residential Real Estate Investing

This is the flip side of homeowners who, during the depression, we're unable to pay for their mortgage payments. Most individuals with tools and knowledge like residential property investment have been able to capitalize on the situation. Real estate has been one of the most significant asset instruments for many people in history for a long time. In the United States, more millionaires were created through real estate investment than in any other industry.

Since the start of the recession in 2012, real estate investors have taken advantage of every opportunity to invest in residential property across the United States. At discount prices up to 55% off the value of the property market. How can you ask how these prices are made? When the recession began, most companies reduced their workers in large numbers, creating a domino effect on the marketplace. Most homeowners started to stop making monthly mortgage payments on their homes after several months of unemployment. Banks and mortgage companies suddenly found themselves more able to manage all at the same time and massive amounts of unpaid mortgage payments on their hands. In an attempt to solve this issue, these mortgage companies and banks started issuing notices of default to homeowners to get homeowners to begin paying back on their loans.

That initiative was unsuccessful, and in fact, many loans occurring some years before the downturn had interest rate changes built-in to the mortgage which was immediately scheduled to raise the mortgage payment to buyers by about $2,000 or more per month, causing more distressed mortgage payments because homeowners were unable to pay the increased mortgage payments. This almost brought the financial system of the United States to a complete standstill that hadn't happened since the 1930's Great Depression. So, with banks and mortgages pursuing their standard hedging practices on delinquent homeowners, this created an ample supply of homes for the property market as a whole at a bad time.

With an unstable housing market, new homeowners were reluctant to take the chance to get wrapped up in the devalued real estate market, property values that had risen from 2004-2008 took a significant drop in value almost overnight. This is where prospects for investment in residential real estate presented themselves. Many of these people had purchased and restored homes through the 2004-2008 boom period and made a lot of money in the process.

So, we are happy to take advantage of this down market with cash new. Banks had to sell this oversupply of properties as they are forced to get these default loans off their books by the US government bank regulators. As the only real buyer in the market, banks started one by one to sell stock to residential real estate investors at high discounted prices. Such buyers, in effect, made home renovations, and as months passed by some prospective homeowners, they began to hear that there were lower prices available on the markets, so they agreed they should take a chance at homeownership. Residential real estate developers began selling their assets to these new homeowners, which they had purchased from the banks at discounts of up to 50%. The new homeowners were pleased because they were able to buy homes that were far cheaper than they could buy the same house just a year before. Now they were getting new updated features that the real estate investor had thrown in like-new stainless steel appliances, improved cabinetry, freshly painted property through the building, and new floors that were used to encourage the homeowner to purify themselves.

The investment segment of residential property started to put more money into the market to buy more discounted properties from the banks. Some houses are sold for profits of up to $300,000 to $400,000 per unit depending on where the apartment was in the state, making an insane profit amounts of money. For such investors in residential property, this was good for the company. This trend holds to this very day, but the banks who figured out how much they made these investors have changed their ways of selling the assets. Massive profits are still open, but in 2009 through 2011, they aren't quite as big as the starting days. Once the word came out how much money was produced for distressed real estate properties, new investors in the reselling real estate market joined the group, many of whom had never been in the real estate business before the recession. If you've ever dreamed about making money outside of your current job, there are still ways in this field to make money at times without the need for your cash or credit.

How to Automate Your Real Estate Investing Business

One thing you'll see quickly when you invest in Real Estate is that there's a lot of work to do to get a deal done, and the weather you're a rehabber or a wholesaler, and you've got to do a lot of work before it's sold. You usually have more time than cash at the start of most shareholder companies, and you end up doing everything yourself to keep down your costs and increase your profits. Heck, marketing itself is costly enough, and if you have little or no money to start with, you're forced to do all you can to get your first contract.

That's fine, and nearly everyone starts that way, but you don't always want to stay that way, even if by doing so, you can make a more significant piece of the pie. But why is this? If I could save money and make more per deal, why wouldn't I want to do it all myself? There's a straightforward reason why you want to pay someone else to do certain things and why working on others is essential to you. The simple answer is not the same as all the tasks of an investment real estate business. Saying the same word in another way, some jobs are simple enough that anyone can do them while others need the ability to think, invent, lead, and communicate.

When you look at any company, the lowest-paid workers are usually the non-skilled workers where there is no specialized training for them to do their job, and those positions pay the least. Anyone can be taught how to clean a toilet: P The middle class of workers usually requires some degree or a unique skill set to do their jobs, and as a result, these workers are paid more. Any corporation's top tier is the people with innovative ideas, management, and communication skills to make it happen. We get paid the most as a result. Your real estate business is the same as any company, so treat it like that! And back to my original question as to why you don't want to do this on your own. Focusing on essential tasks and contracting out the bottom and eventually, middle-level tasks for others to do is simply more productive. This is attributable to something called "hourly pay." When you spread your time doing all aspects of the business, you take your hourly wage and average it from the whole pie. If, on the other hand, you only perform the essential tasks and contract the rest at a low price, you will produce more, and your hourly wage will rise. This is the main difference between a sole owner and a businessman and why the businessman ends up making money. I don't know about you, but I got to make money and have a ton of free time in this business!

Let me give you an excellent example of what I'm thinking about. My husband and I primarily sell the MLS and Craigslist in two different locations to find all of our offers. Both of these places are necessarily free to market (yes, I know the MLS costs money every year, but let's say it's free from there... deal? after the fee is paid). And, every day we can spend hours sending lowball deals to the MLS and advertising on Craigslist to get people to call in. Then every day, we can spend hours dealing with Realtors ' answers and sellers ' calls. All you need to find a deal, and that's when it all happens at once! Now you're having to do daily tasks like putting up advertisements and making offers on the MLS, coping with emails and calls in addition to putting together the deal so that you can either sell or rehabilitate it. What's most likely to happen is that the lower tier activities cease while you're focused on the tasks that make you money, and when you make that money, you've got to start all over again... blah: P!

So that's what I suggest ;) Hire a Virtual Assistant after you make your first or even second deal, and you've got some money to play with now! When we did that our production skyrocketed and there was a decrease in the amount of work we had to do... and all that work was the tedious work we hated doing! Now we have a lady over in India who works for $2.25 an hour with a Masters' degree making offers on the

MLS. Have you heard me there... she's got a Master Dang, and she's working for $2.25 an hour!

Try to see if you can get a homeless man to work for the cheap one. Ha! Even if you could bet a month's wages, he wouldn't put in the same effort and enthusiasm as the lady with her degree we have in India;) She's extraordinarily productive and very smart and can send 50-60 offers to the MLS within 2 hours. We started working 10 hours a week with her, and she was worth her gold weight! Think about it, and we've got about 250-300 deals for about $25 each week. We made her do more research as time went by, while we focused on the creative tasks (which are also more enjoyable and take less time)... high!

Necessarily, Virtual Assistants are people who can perform any function you request of them that can be done on an internet-connected device. Someone who sends an offer to the MLS or places an ad on Craigslist does NOT have to be in my office, nor do I have to see them know they are doing their job. We let her use our company email to send deals, and we can track her progress by merely checking the sent folder to see what she's doing... so limited oversight. So, anywhere in the world, this person can be! How many of us wanted to work with our jobs from home, but it never seemed that the bosses were on board for it?

We can now be the "hot" boss and as a result, reap the rewards! You can do all the menial tasks once you have someone on board and let you concentrate on the things that will make you money, like bringing together buyers and sellers! The larger you get, the more tasks you need your Virtual Assistant to delegate. You can eventually get an "apprentice" real estate investor who can do everything you need, including managing your Virtual Assistant. A wage plus a percentage of profits can be paid to him.

Mortgages For Real Estate Investments

If you need to obtain a mortgage for your first real estate investment property, take your time to look at the various options available. Of course, having great credit helps. The good your reputation is, the more likely you are to get the loan you need. Here are some options for securing a mortgage loan for your property:

Fixed mortgage
A fixed mortgage usually lasts 30 years and does not adjust, hence the name "fixed rate." This is the mortgage loan's wife. Real estate investors have only been able to obtain this kind of loan for a long time. When they get a fixed mortgage loan, if

they pay it off sooner, it comes with a fixed rate that will continue for the term of 30 years or less. The loan will be deemed to be paid in full by the end of the e30-year term. The monthly loan payments are applied to the interest of the loan in the early years. We are finally added to the inner balance as the years go by. This is about investors ' most manageable loan to manage as the terms are plain.

Usually, as you continue to pay off, you will not find anything unexpected down the road. Perhaps real estate investor will for a long time with a lot of debt. The real estate investment emphasis is on creating wealth, not having financial liabilities at all times. As investors gain wealth from investing in real estate, they will enjoy it as they keep investing in more properties.

Zero Investment (No-Money Down Loans)

This is another type of mortgage loan that property investors can use. They're not going to have a problem trying to get information about this type of loan because they're always being advertised somewhere. Sometimes it can be claimed as one of the best loans since bread has been sliced. It is critical, however, that borrowers are aware of the risks involved in obtaining such a loan.

Investors in real estate can obtain this type of loan by securing a 100% mortgage, or they can accomplish what is called a "piggyback" mortgage. A piggyback loan is when two mortgages are backed and brought together by the lender at the same time.

The investor gets a bonus with a piggyback mortgage by not having to downplay at the closing process. The shareholder can also benefit from earning the highest amount of interest allowed to be included as a deduction in their taxes.

Being a borrower, you're not always sure to get the whole amount funded for the loan. There are many banks and other creditors that do not provide the full 100%. If some want to provide the entire lot, by including higher interest rates, they will get their share. That way, because you wouldn't have made a down payment, they would protect themselves.

The mortgage payments will be higher than usual, as with anything else that is zero-down. This kind of loan can hurt you in the long run if you don't have a lot of money as a financial backup. Getting a stable cash flow would take you longer because you'd pay a more significant amount of mortgage payments. So, you might want to think a little harder than others about this loan opportunity.

A zero-down loan, however, could still work to secure an investment property for you. Whether or not you are willing and capable of taking the risk is up to you.

Adjustable mortgage rate

Adjustable mortgage loans or ARMs are almost as popular as fixed mortgages, as they are commonly known. Investors in real estate are also likely to use these. When you agree on this mortgage, a fixed interest rate can be guaranteed.

A variable rate of interest is the rate paid by borrowers, and it often fluctuates. The rates change following the market interest rate increases or decreases during that period.

It would continue for a couple of years with a fixed rate. Then it would go into a cycle of the parameter. This ensures that your loan rate (and monthly payment) is subject to change each year after the fixed-rate duration is over.

With that, many ARMs have a stopping point as to how much they can adjust. With this loan, as long as you have it, the rate may increase or decrease to a certain amount.

Initially, this form of loan may include a low-interest rate. This would appeal to some real estate investors as they may not want to hang on to the property for an extended period.

Often, investors can take the opportunity to get in on them if interest rates fall. This loan, on the other hand, is very risky.

The investor will have to go with the flow when interest rates rise.

The bad thing about this is, when the rates will rise, they won't know in advance. In reality, ARMs can be an uncertain thing because you don't know how much money you're going to keep paying because of the fluctuations that is constant.

Interest Only Loan

Another credit in the interest-only mortgage loan that is right for the real estate investor. Investors can use this fund when it is difficult to obtain a positive cash flow. Typically this occurs when the property's price. Has increased.

Some investors usually receive interest-only loans if they don't want negative cash flow, if they're going to use the cash for something else, or if they're planning to flip into the property for a future date.

If an investor has this kind of mortgage loan, for a certain period, they can hold off on principal payments. Usually, it's not more than 10 years, but it might be less. During this period, the investor will only pay the interest and nothing else. The debt will be amortized again to get rid of the balance in the future after the time of paying only the interest has passed. The investor ends up paying a higher payment for mortgage loans. The borrower can handle this situation in several ways:

selling their assets, sticking to the higher payment, or attempting to refinance.

Balloon mortgage

Using a balloons mortgage are not one of the most popular types of mortgages loans, then the real estate investor has used it. Using more time than the actual loan term, this mortgage increases. The investor ends up paying less.

At the end of the term, though, there will be a balance to be paid in full by the lender or to refinance the loan. If the buyer is unable to pay the total lump sum or seek refinancing, the investor must ultimately sell the property.

Although, in the beginning, the investor may end up being the loser if they are unable to pay off the entire refinance or balance. Plus, the borrower would have to cope with an increase in interest rates with refinancing, plus costs of refinancing. That's just more money coming out of your wallet than you need.

Conclusion

Congratulations! You have gotten to the end of this fantastic journey. This says a lot about how serious you are about becoming a real investor, and you've made a good choice by trying to know more from this book. All that you've read will help you succeed in the real estate industry. The level of commitment and interest you have shown so far will help you throughout your journey into the real estate world. You'll come across various challenges and difficulties, but your determination will get you going. You'll also be exposed to some risks, but you'll scale through since you're well prepared for them.

Ensure you come up with a good plan and make necessary findings before buying any property to avoid problems later. Challenges will always come up, but they will be minimal when you do your due diligence.

If you're a first-time investor, do not rely on your knowledge alone, as this can be disastrous in the long run. Work with the right set of people to save yourself from various problems that may arise along the line. Do all you can to get good hands and employ the help of professionals. As you work with them and invest in more and more properties, you'll have a better understanding of what works and what doesn't work.

Read, understand, and digest the information in this book and repeat the process. Apply it in your real estate experiences and see yourself succeed in this beautiful world of opportunities. Real estate investment isn't a new trend. It has been around for a long time and is one of the most popular businesses around the world these days. You probably have heard about it a lot of times. It is a simple means of making cash, especially when you are flipping properties. Your interest in real estate might have been triggered by an advert on TV, or from a close friend earning quite an income from investing in real estate. Okay, so you have developed an interest in it, but now the problem is: you don't know how to go about it or where to start.

You are not alone in this. Many have been and are still in your shoes or worse; they were not successful when they first tried investing in real estate, while others have started hitting it big. So, where did they go wrong? What was their mistake? Why did some succeed where others were unable to? How can one be successful in real estate?

If you are here, you are on the right route. There are many books on how to invest in real estate, but for some reason, you have chosen to read this book. You are in luck! This book answers all of the questions above and covers all of the vital information for anyone who wants to begin investing in real estate. By reading this book, you are taking a giant leap towards being successful in this venture.

In this book, you will learn everything about real estate investment; Its pros and cons, everything! You will be provided with insights on the various forms of profitable real estate investments, how to source for finance, and how to make offers. You will gain the knowledge needed in investing in real estate for profit. You will also learn about some of the popular real estate myths that have managed to stop many individuals from being as successful as they are supposed to be. While there will be hurdles and obstacles ahead, you will be armed with a detailed understanding of everything you require to scale through them.

CPSIA information can be obtained
at www.ICGtesting.com
Printed in the USA
BVHW041719230221
600894BV00015B/1590

9 781801 912525